Spanish
Activity Book

for ages 5-7

This CGP book has bags of fun activities
to build up children's knowledge and confidence.

There's even online audio for all the key words — perfect
for developing listening skills and pronunciation. Enjoy!

This book is a brilliant way to help children learn Spanish vocabulary.

To access online audio of all the vocabulary in this book, head to cgpbooks.co.uk/primary-spanish-audio or scan this QR code on your smartphone.

Spanish Vocabulary

Published by CGP

Editors:
Siân Butler, Ilana Pearce, Hannah Roscoe, Hayley Shaw, Jennifer Underwood

With thanks to Becca Lakin for the proofreading.

With thanks to Jade Sim for the copyright research.

ISBN: 978 1 83774 009 3

Printed by Elanders Ltd, Newcastle upon Tyne.
Graphics used on the cover and throughout the book © Educlips 2022
Cover design concept by emc design ltd.

Text, design, layout and original illustrations © Coordination Group Publications Ltd. (CGP) 2022
All rights reserved.

Photocopying this book is not permitted, even if you have a CLA licence.
Extra copies are available from CGP with next day delivery • 0800 1712 712 • www.cgpbooks.co.uk

Contents

Hello!	2
How are you?	4
What is your name?	6
Numbers	8
Colours	10
My family	12
Animals	14
Clothes	16
Puzzle: Snowy shuffle	18
What do you like doing?	20
Food	22
In my pencil case	24
Where do you live?	26
My house	28
Do you remember?	30
Race through the rainforest	32
Vocabulary	33
Answers	35

Hello!

How It Works

This is how you say 'hello' and 'goodbye' in Spanish.

¡Hola! Hello!
¡Adiós! Goodbye!

¡Hola! Hello!
¡Adiós! Goodbye!

Now Try These

1. Circle the words that mean 'hello'.
   Underline the ones that mean 'goodbye'.

¡Hola!

¡Adiós!

¡Adiós!

¡Hola!

2. Draw a line that joins all the letters together to spell 'adiós'.

C D S E
A I H Ó

3. Colour in the letters to spell out 'hola'.

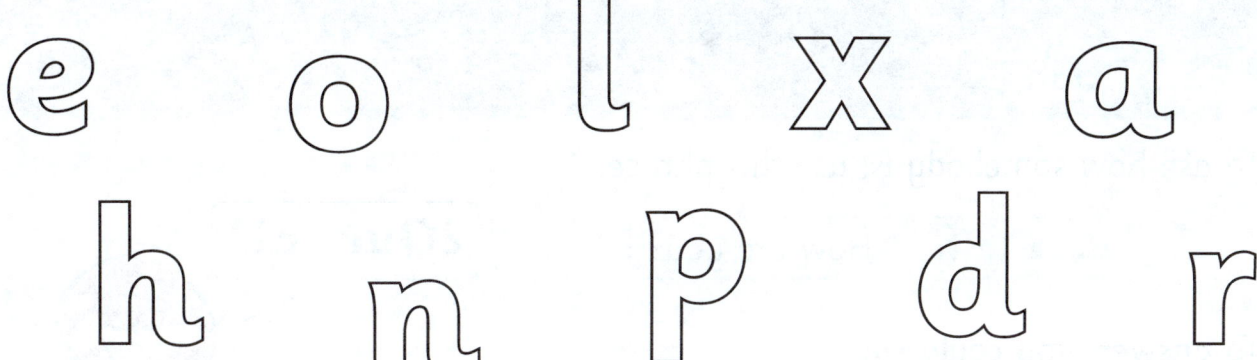

4. Complete the sentences below in English.

Marco is saying ....

Aaliyah is saying ....

An Extra Challenge

Aarón has bumped into his friend Valeria in the park.
Complete their conversation, and practise saying these greetings out loud.

Are you a pro at saying hello?
Put a tick in one of the boxes.

How are you?

How It Works

To ask how somebody is, use this phrase.

¿Qué tal? How are you?

To answer, you could say:

Bien, gracias. I'm well, thank you.

Bastante bien. Quite well.

Now Try These

1. Colour the speech bubbles that say 'How are you?' in blue. Colour the ones that say 'I'm fine, thank you.' in pink.

2. Feng has asked Lily how she is. Complete Lily's speech bubble so that she says "quite well" in Spanish.

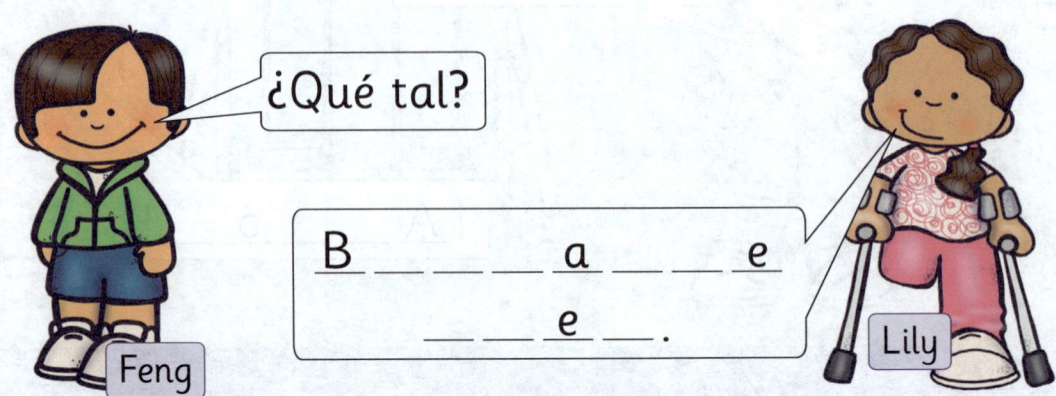

B _ _ _ a _ _ e
_ _ e _.

3. Colour in the letters and punctuation which spell out '¿Qué tal?'.

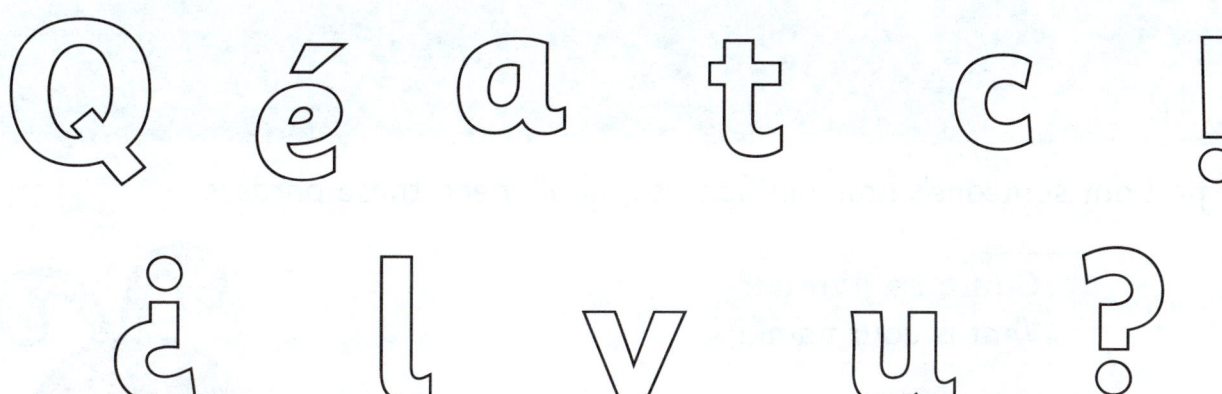

4. Fill in the blanks to finish the conversation.

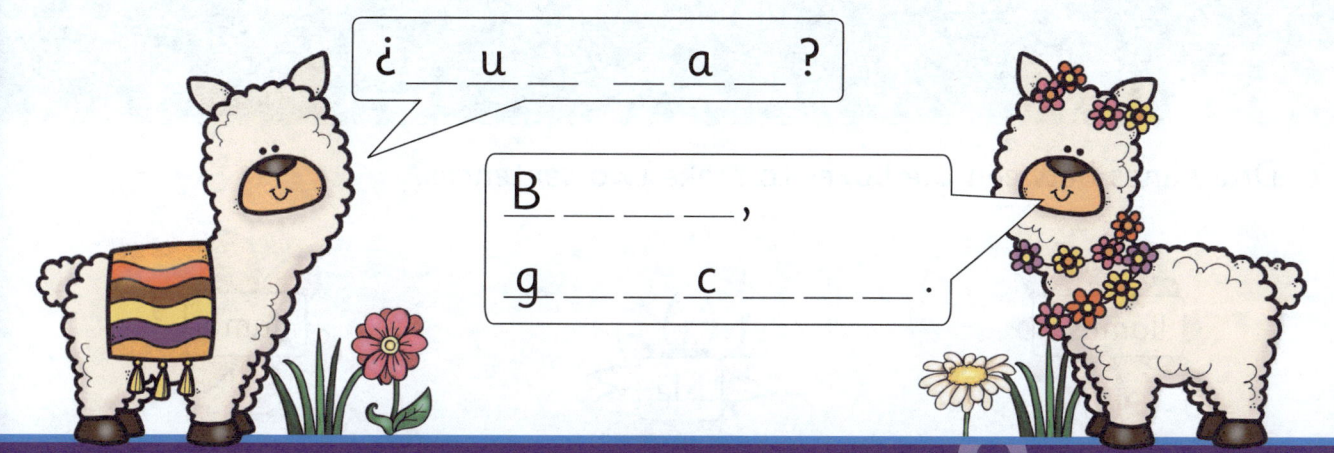

¿_ u _ _ _ a _ ?

B_ _ _ _ _,
g_ _ _ _ c_ _ _ _ _.

An Extra Challenge

Esteban has tried to answer Nerea's question, but he has got confused. Can you write his answer in the correct order? Then, answer the question yourself.

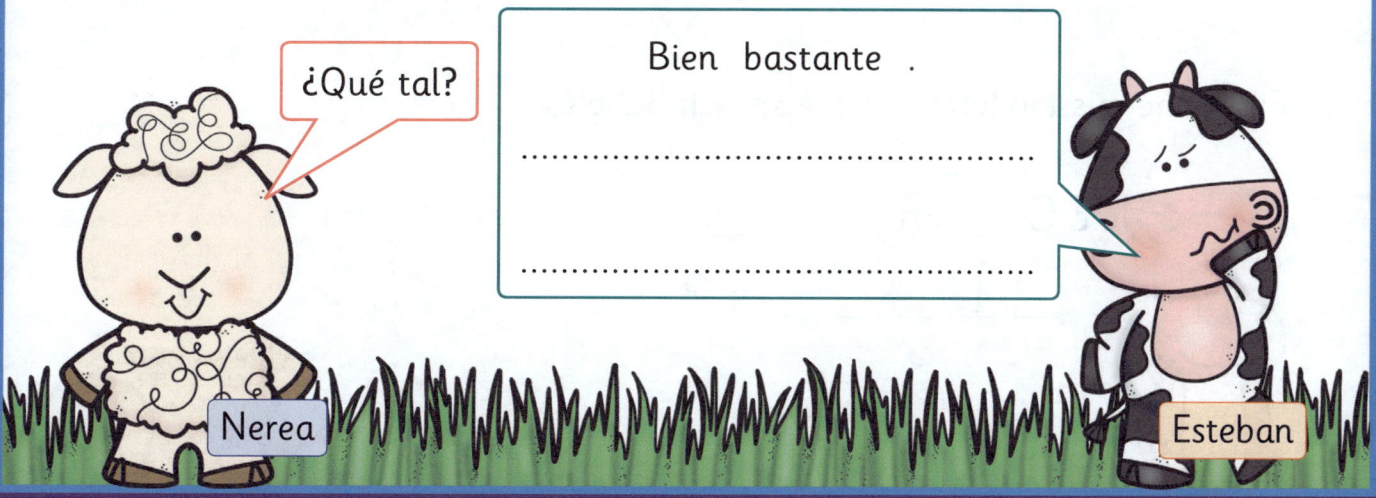

¿Qué tal?

Bien   bastante   .

How do you feel about these pages? Put a tick in a box.

What is your name?

How It Works

To find out someone's name in Spanish, you'll need these phrases.

¿Cómo te llamas?
What is your name?

Me llamo...
My name is...

Now Try These

1. Draw lines between the boxes to make two sentences.

2. Fill in the missing letters in the speech bubbles.

¿C _ m _ _ e
_ l _ _ _ _ s ?

M _ _ _ a _
A b b y .

3. Circle the correct Spanish words to match each English sign.

Hello!
¿Cómo te llamas?
¿Qué tal?
¡Hola!

How are you?
Me llamo
¡Adiós!
¿Qué tal?

My name is
¡Adiós!
Me llamo
¿Cómo te llamas?

4. Xavier has asked Zarah a question. Rewrite her answer with the words in the correct order.

¿Cómo te llamas? — Xavier

llamo Zarah Me.

....

 Zarah

An Extra Challenge

Gerald has sent you a secret message in Spanish. To find out what it says, cross out the blue boxes to see what is left. Can you write down what it means in English on the lines below?

¿ C a ó m l o   t u e
l l u a e m a t s ?

....

....

Is your name 'Spanish star'?
Put a tick in one of the boxes.

7

Numbers

How It Works

Here are the numbers from one to ten in Spanish.

los números	numbers

uno	one
dos	two
tres	three
cuatro	four
cinco	five

seis	six
siete	seven
ocho	eight
nueve	nine
diez	ten

Now Try These

1. Write the Spanish word for each number below.

7 ....siete........ **1** ....

3 .... **4** ....

8 .... **6** ....

2. Draw lines to match the numbers to the Spanish words.

4   diez   5   dos   9

cinco   2   nueve   10   cuatro

3. Count how many items there are in each group.
   Write the number in Spanish in the box.

   a) ....

   b) ....

   c) ....

   d) ....

An Extra Challenge

Penelope the pet shop owner wants to make sure she has the right amount of fish in each bowl. Can you draw the correct number of fish?

cinco

dos

tres

Are you a counting champion?
Tick one of the boxes.

Colours

How It Works

Here are some words to talk about colours in Spanish.

los colores colours

 **rojo** red

 **verde** green

 **blanco** white

 **azul** blue

 **amarillo** yellow

 **negro** black

Now Try These

1. Colour in the icing to match the label on each cupcake.

2. Write the English words next to the Spanish words.

verde ___ ___ ___ ___ ___

rojo ___ ___ ___

negro ___ ___ ___ ___ ___

azul ___ ___ ___ ___

blanco ___ ___ ___ ___ ___

amarillo ___ ___ ___ ___ ___ ___

3. Label the items with the correct colour in Spanish.

4. Find the Spanish words for the colours in the wordsearch.

q	a	s	e	g	l	g	p	g	f
v	r	b	l	a	n	c	o	a	m
e	o	n	k	g	d	a	h	z	x
r	j	g	n	e	g	r	o	u	g
d	o	e	o	f	b	o	g	l	h
e	e	g	j	v	p	f	j	g	r
g	m	a	m	a	r	i	l	l	o

blanco   verde
negro   amarillo
azul   rojo

An Extra Challenge

The unicorns are getting ready for a party. They've each brought some decorations with them. Write the colour of each object in Spanish on the lines below.

balloons: ....

party hats: ....

cake icing: ....

Are you a colour whizz?
Tick a box to show how you did.

11

My family

How It Works

To talk about your family in Spanish, you'll need these words.

- **mi familia** — my family
- **yo** — me
- **mi madre** — my mother
- **mi abuela** — my grandmother
- **mi hermano** — my brother
- **mi abuelo** — my grandfather
- **mi padre** — my father
- **mi hermana** — my sister

Now Try These

1. For each picture, colour in the family member that is mentioned.

Mi madre.

Mi abuelo.

2. Unscramble the letters to make the names of family members.

i m a r e
h m a n

....

....

m u i e
a b a l

i m m a
e r d

....

....

m p a
i r d e

An Extra Challenge

Aurelia and Mo are talking about their families and showing each other photographs. Can you finish the sentences below?

mi padre (Amir)   mi madre (Yasmeen)   mi abuelo (Terrence)

mi hermana (Amber)   Mo   Aurelia   mi abuela (Doria)

Mo's ....   Aurelia's ....
is called Yasmeen.   is called Terrence.

Do you feel fantastic about family vocabulary? Tick a box.

Animals

How It Works

Use these words to talk about animals.

 los animales animals

 **el perro** dog    **el pájaro** bird    **el conejo** rabbit    **el pez** fish

 **el caballo** horse    **el hámster** hamster    **el gato** cat

Now Try These

1. Write the Spanish word for the animal that lives in each of these places.

....

2. Draw a picture in each frame for the words below.

el caballo   el perro   el conejo

3. Draw lines to connect each animal to the correct Spanish word.

el conejo

el pájaro

el gato

el pez

An Extra Challenge

Some of the farmer's pets have escaped. Can you bring them home by finding your way through the maze and writing the animals in the order you meet them?

1. el conejo
2. ....
3. ....
4. ....
5. ....
6. ....
7. ....

Did these pages make you feel like the top dog? Tick a box.

Clothes

How It Works

If you want to talk about clothes in Spanish, you'll need these words.

la ropa — clothes

 la falda — skirt
 la camiseta — T-shirt
 el jersey — jumper
 el vestido — dress

 los pantalones — trousers
 los zapatos — shoes
 los calcetines — socks

Now Try These

1. Write the English word for each of these Spanish words.

   la falda → _ _ _ _ _ _

   los zapatos → _ _ _ _ _ _

   el vestido → _ _ _ _ _ _

   los pantalones → _ _ _ _ _ _ _ _

2. Colour in each item of clothing to match its label.

la falda roja   los pantalones verdes   la camiseta azul

3. Draw lines to match each word to the correct item of clothing. Cross out any words you don't need.

la camiseta

el jersey

los pantalones

los calcetines

la falda

los zapatos

4. Colour in the correct spelling of each Spanish word.

a) la falda — la falde

d) los zepatos — los zapatos

b) el jesey — el jersey

e) el vestio — el vestido

c) la camiseta — la camasita

f) los pantalones — los pantalanes

An Extra Challenge

Khadija is going to a party. Write the Spanish words for the clothes she is wearing. Then, write a list of clothes that you are wearing.

Khadija

....

....

....

Khadija

Are you dressed for Spanish success? Tick a box.

Snowy shuffle

Luisa, Manuel and Camila have been shopping, but on the way home, they were caught in a snowstorm and their things got mixed up! They need help sorting out their items. Can you draw lines to connect each animal to the items on their shopping list?

Luisa

1. los zapatos rojos
2. el lápiz
3. el chocolate

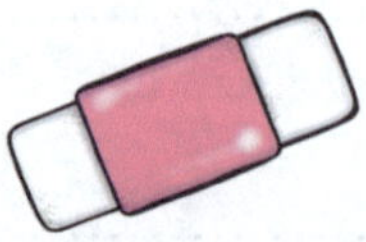

What do you like doing?

How It Works

Read these words and phrases, then answer the questions below.

¿Qué te gusta hacer?
What do you like doing?

Me gusta... I like...

...jugar al fútbol
...playing football

...ver la tele
...watching TV

...bailar
...dancing

...leer
...reading

...nadar
...swimming

...escuchar música
...listening to music

Now Try These

1. Draw lines to match each sentence to the correct picture.

   Me gusta leer.

   Me gusta ver la tele.

   Me gusta jugar al fútbol.

2. Complete the English sentences below about Axel and Carys.

    Me gusta leer.

    Me gusta nadar.

   Axel likes ....   Carys likes ....

3. Circle the pictures to show what Thiago likes to do.

   ¡Hola! Me gusta escuchar música, leer, jugar al fútbol y nadar.

An Extra Challenge

Follow the lines with a pencil to find out what each person likes to do. Match their name with the correct Spanish sentence. Then, write what you like to do.

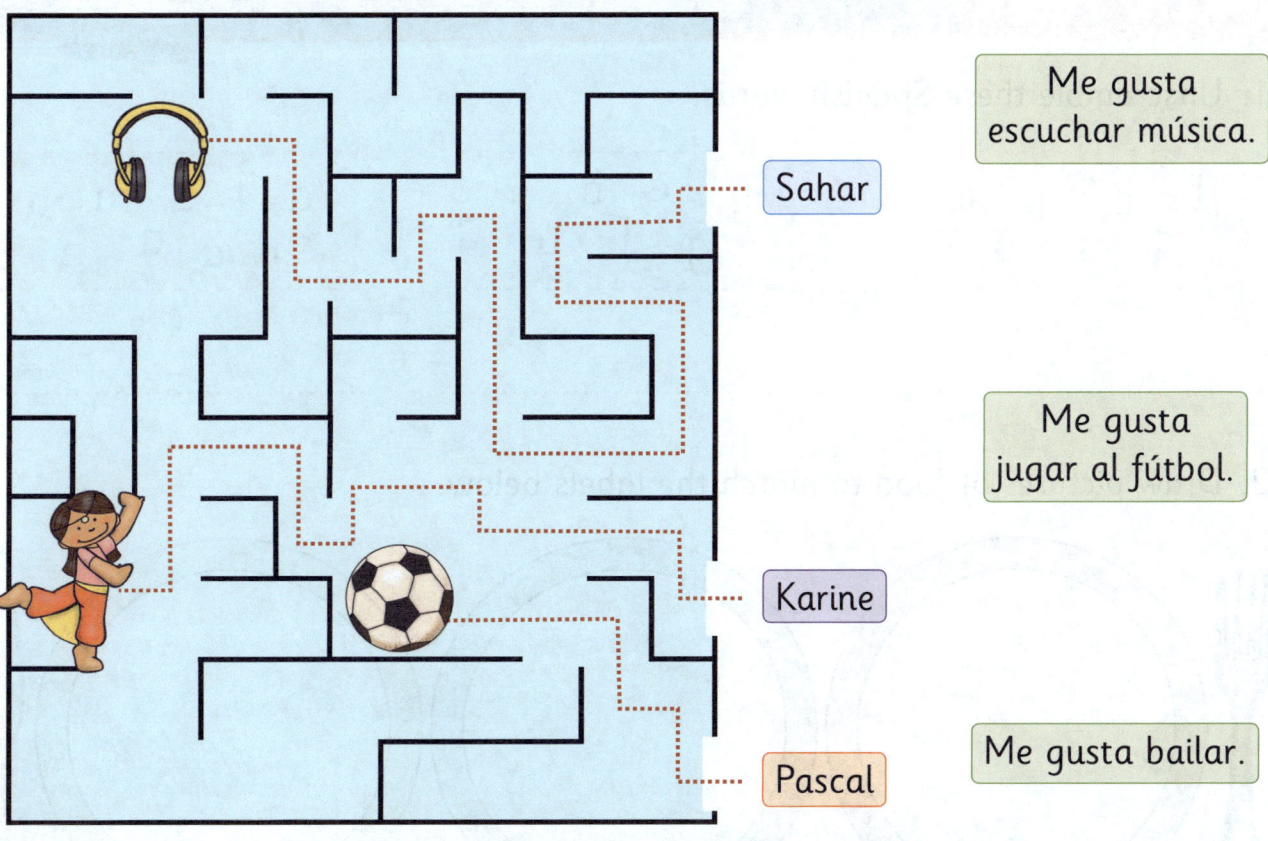

Did you like learning about this topic? Put a tick in a box.

Food

How It Works

If you want to talk about food, you'll need these words.

la comida food

la manzana apple

las patatas fritas chips

los espaguetis spaghetti

el yogur yoghurt

el chocolate chocolate

el bocadillo sandwich

el queso cheese

Now Try These

1. Unscramble these Spanish words.

   | l e u e q s o | y e o r g l u | a l z m a n a a n |

   ....

2. Draw pictures of food to match the labels below.

las patatas fritas

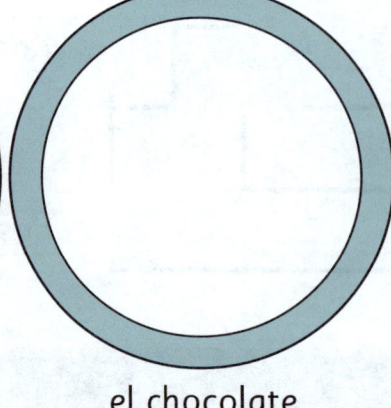
el chocolate

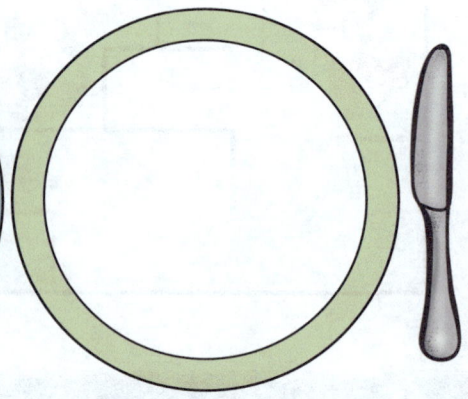
los espaguetis

3. Circle the correct picture for each word.

4. Colour in the foods that match the words below.

An Extra Challenge

Chef Arif has hidden a secret cake ingredient in English in his recipe book. Can you help him reveal it? Fill in the gaps in each word, then use the letters in the green circles to spell out the ingredient.

The ingredient is:

....

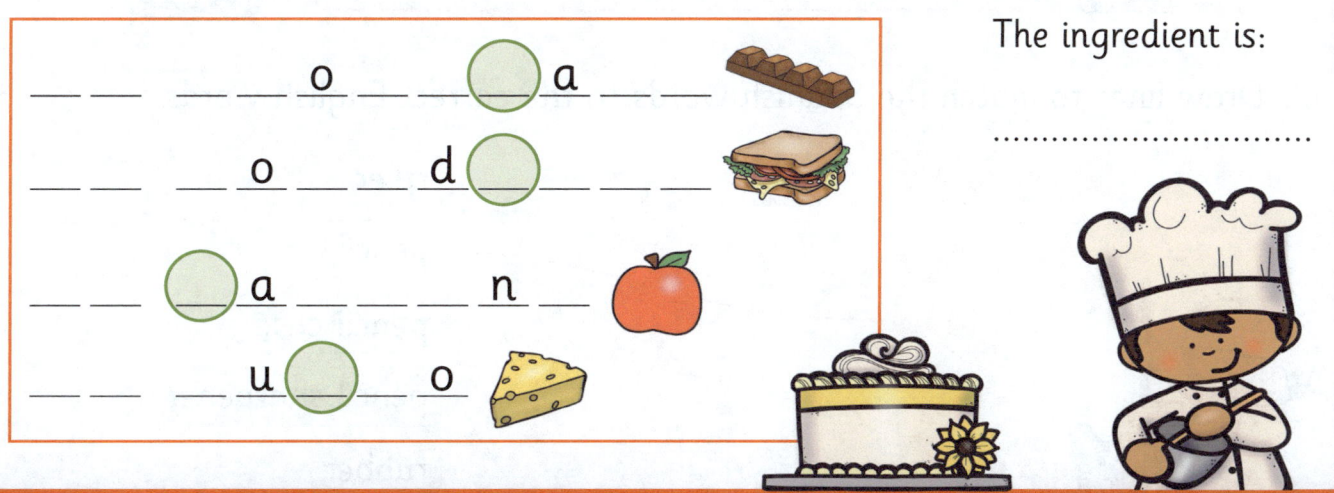

Are you the big cheese when it comes to food in Spanish?

In my pencil case

How It Works

Use these words to talk about the items in your pencil case.

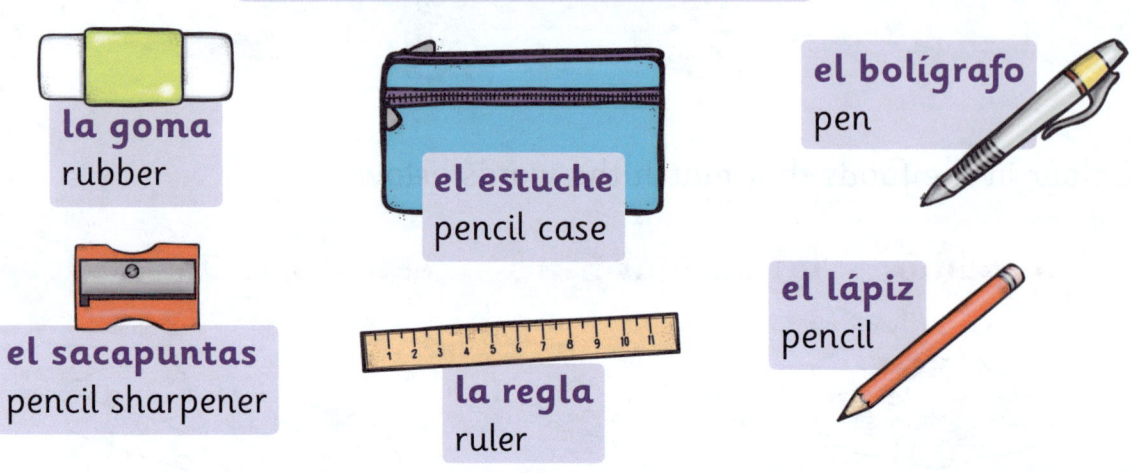

en mi estuche in my pencil case

- **la goma** rubber
- **el estuche** pencil case
- **el bolígrafo** pen
- **el sacapuntas** pencil sharpener
- **la regla** ruler
- **el lápiz** pencil

Now Try These

1. Colour the items you might find in a pencil case.

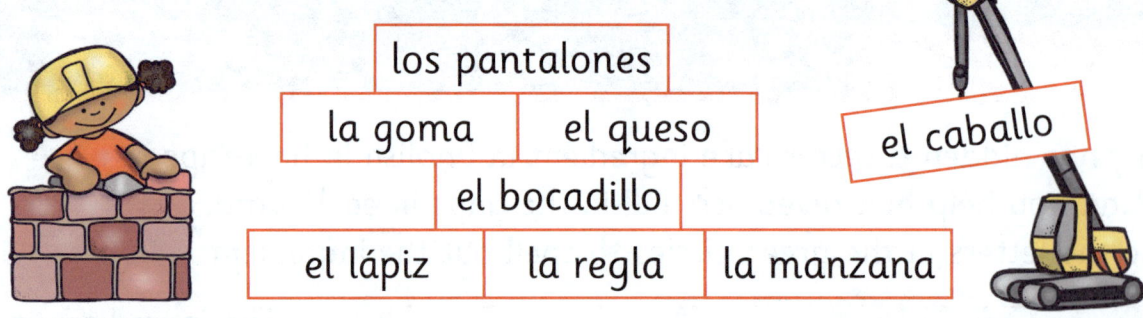

- los pantalones
- la goma
- el queso
- el caballo
- el bocadillo
- el lápiz
- la regla
- la manzana

2. Draw lines to match the Spanish words to the correct English words.

el bolígrafo	ruler
el sacapuntas	pencil
el lápiz	pencil case
la regla	pencil sharpener
el estuche	rubber
la goma	pen

3. Write the Spanish words for each of these pictures.

   a) _ a _ e _ _ _

   b) _ _ g _ _ _ _

   Remember! You need to put either 'el' or 'la' before each of these words.

   c) e _ _ _ l _ _ a _ _

An Extra Challenge

Fergus is packing his pencil case for school. Can you help him find everything he needs? Draw a path to his pencil case by passing through the items in the order that Fergus says them. Then, make a list of what's in your pencil case.

el bolígrafo, la regla azul, el bolígrafo, la goma, el lápiz, el sacapuntas, la regla verde

Did you manage to crack the pencil case? Tick a box.

Where do you live?

How It Works

To talk about where you live, you'll need these phrases.

¿Dónde vives?
Where do you live?

Vivo...
I live...

...en un castillo
...in a castle

...en una casa
...in a house

...en un piso
...in a flat

...en el campo
...in the countryside

...cerca del mar
...by the sea

...en la ciudad
...in the city / town

Now Try These

1. Draw a line to match each picture to the correct sentence.

Vivo en una casa.

Vivo cerca del mar.

Vivo en el campo.

Vivo en un castillo.

Vivo en la ciudad.

2. Read what each person is saying.
   Colour the correct picture to show where they live.

   "Vivo en la ciudad."

   "Vivo en el campo."

   "Vivo cerca del mar."

An Extra Challenge

Flora is telling you where she lives. Draw a picture to show what she's saying, then answer her question below.

"Vivo en una casa en el campo."

"¿Dónde vives?"

Vivo ....

Are you a whizz at talking about where you live in Spanish?

My house

How It Works

Here are the Spanish words for some rooms you can find in a house.

mi casa — my house
el dormitorio — the bedroom
el cuarto de baño — the bathroom
la cocina — the kitchen
el comedor — the dining room
el salón — the living room

Now Try These

1. Match the Spanish words to the correct English words.

   el cuarto de baño   el salón   the dining room
   the bedroom   the living room
   la cocina   the kitchen   el dormitorio
   el comedor   the bathroom

2. Unscramble these Spanish words.

   Remember! Don't forget 'el' or 'la'.

   s a l   l n e ó
   c e r m   l o d e o
   l i a c   o c n a

   ....

3. Fill in the gaps to spell the room where you might find each object.

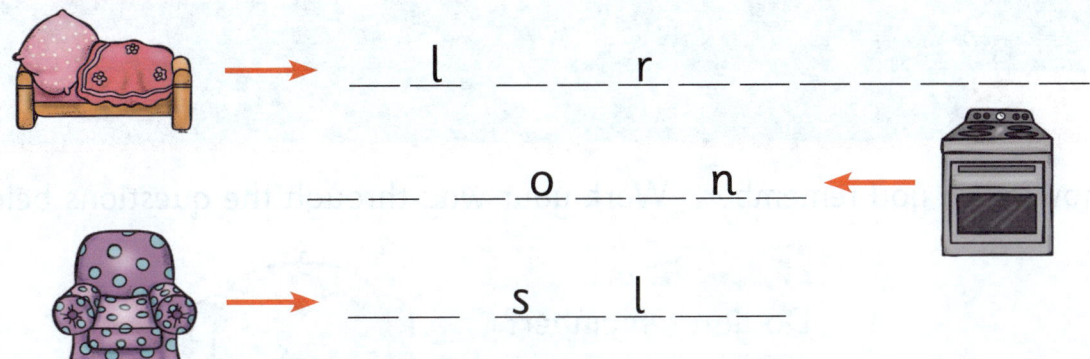

__ l __ __ r __ __ __ __ __ __

__ __ __ __ o __ n __ __

__ __ __ s __ l __ __

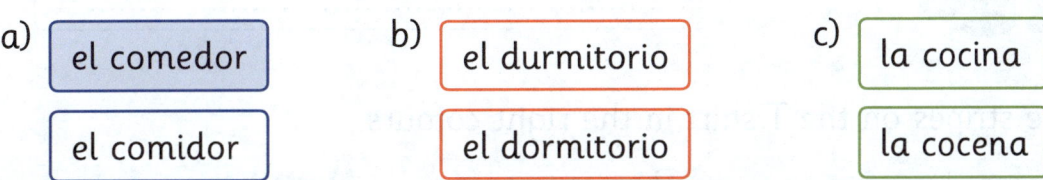

4. Colour the words that you need to say 'the bathroom' in red, and the words to say 'the dining room' in blue. Leave any words you don't need blank.

el   cuarto   comedor

casa   de   el   baño   la

5. Colour in the correct spelling of each Spanish word.

a) el comedor / el comidor

b) el durmitorio / el dormitorio

c) la cocina / la cocena

An Extra Challenge

Immy is getting ready to leave the house, but she's forgotten some important items. Can you write the Spanish words for the rooms she needs to visit?

Her key is in the living room.

....

Her glasses are in the bedroom.

....

Her water bottle is in the kitchen.

....

Did these pages make you feel at home? Tick one of the boxes.

Do you remember?

How It Works

Let's see how much you remember. Work your way through the questions below.

¿Recuerdas?
Do you remember?

Now Try These

1. What is your name? **¿Cómo te llamas?**
   Write a reply, in Spanish, in the gaps below.

   _ e   _ l _ _ _ _

   ....

2. Colour the stripes on the T-shirt in the right colours.

   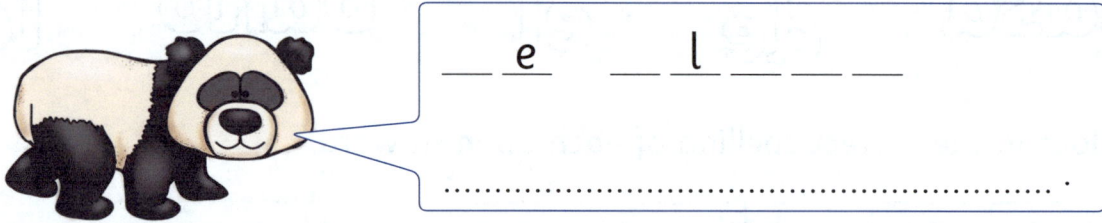

   - azul
   - blanco
   - rojo
   - amarillo
   - verde
   - negro

3. Circle the correct Spanish words to match each English sign.

   the rabbit
   - el queso
   - el jersey
   - el conejo
   - el estuche

   the kitchen
   - la manzana
   - el salón
   - el bolígrafo
   - la cocina

   goodbye
   - adiós
   - me llamo
   - buenas tardes

30

4. Colour in the words for the clothes you are wearing.

los pantalones el jersey
el vestido los calcetines
la camiseta la falda
los zapatos

5. Circle the three foods that the goat is thinking about.

el chocolate

las patatas fritas

el queso

el yogur

la manzana

el bocadillo

An Extra Challenge

A diver has met a Spanish crab on the seabed. Can you draw a picture and label it to help the diver understand what the crab is saying?

Me llamo Diego. Vivo en una casa.

Did your marvellous memory help you master these pages?

Race through the rainforest

You'll need a counter for each player and a dice. Place your counters on the first square and take it in turns to roll the dice once. Follow the instructions when you land on them.

Vocabulary

Hello! — ¡Hola!

hola	hello
adiós	goodbye

How are you? — ¿Qué tal?

Bien, gracias.	I'm well, thank you.
Bastante bien.	Quite well.

What is your name? — ¿Cómo te llamas?

Me llamo...	My name is...

Numbers — Los números

uno	1	cinco	5	ocho	8
dos	2	seis	6	nueve	9
tres	3	siete	7	diez	10
cuatro	4				

Colours — Los colores

rojo	red	blanco	white	amarillo	yellow
verde	green	azul	blue	negro	black

My family — Mi familia

yo	me	mi padre	my father
mi madre	my mother	mi abuelo	my grandfather
mi abuela	my grandmother	mi hermano	my brother
mi hermana	my sister		

Animals — Los animales

el perro	dog	el caballo	horse
el pájaro	bird	el hámster	hamster
el conejo	rabbit	el gato	cat
el pez	fish		

Vocabulary

Clothes — La ropa

la falda	skirt	los pantalones	trousers
la camiseta	T-shirt	los zapatos	shoes
el jersey	jumper	los calcetines	socks
el vestido	dress		

What do you like doing? — ¿Qué te gustar hacer?

Me gusta...	I like...	leer	reading
jugar al fútbol	playing football	nadar	swimming
ver la tele	watching TV	bailar	dancing
escuchar música	listening to music		

Food — La comida

la manzana	apple	el chocolate	chocolate
las patatas fritas	chips	el bocadillo	sandwich
los espaguetis	spaghetti	el queso	cheese
el yogur	yoghurt		

In my pencil case — En mi estuche

la goma	rubber	el sacapuntas	pencil sharpener
el estuche	pencil case	la regla	ruler
el bolígrafo	pen	el lápiz	pencil

Where do you live? — ¿Dónde vives?

Vivo...	I live...	en el campo	in the countryside
en una casa	in a house	en la ciudad	in the city / town
en un castillo	in a castle	cerca del mar	by the sea
en un piso	in a flat		

My house — Mi casa

el dormitorio	the bedroom
el cuarto de baño	the bathroom
la cocina	the kitchen
el comedor	the dining room
el salón	the living room

Answers

Pages 2-3 — Hello!

1.

2.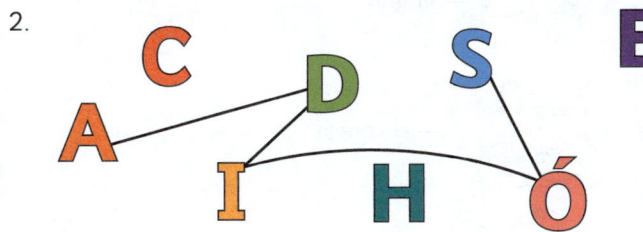

3. You should have coloured in: h, o, l, a.

4. Marco is saying <u>hello</u>.
   Aaliyah is saying <u>goodbye</u>.

   An Extra Challenge
   ¡Hola!
   ¡Adiós!

Pages 4-5 — How are you?

1. The speech bubbles that say '¿Qué tal?' should be coloured in blue.
   The speech bubbles that say 'Bien, gracias.' should be coloured in pink.

2. Bastante bien.

3. You should have coloured in: ¿, Q, u, é, t, a, l, ?.

4. ¿Qué tal?
   Bien, gracias.

   An Extra Challenge
   The correct order is: Bastante bien.

Pages 6-7 — What is your name?

1. You should have made the sentences:
   ¿Cómo te llamas?
   Me llamo Paul.

2. ¿Cómo te llamas?
   Me llamo Abby.

3. You should have circled: ¡Hola!, ¿Qué tal?, Me llamo.

4. The correct order is: Me llamo Zarah.

   An Extra Challenge
   You should have written: What is your name?

Pages 8-9 — Numbers

1. 3 — tres
   8 — ocho
   1 — uno
   4 — cuatro
   6 — seis

2. You should have matched:
   4 — cuatro
   2 — dos
   10 — diez
   9 — nueve

3. a) ocho
   b) cinco
   c) siete
   d) cuatro

   An Extra Challenge
   Any suitable drawing of the correct number of fish, e.g.
   dos:
   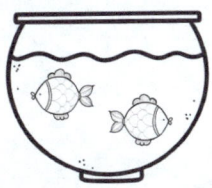

Pages 10-11 — Colours

1.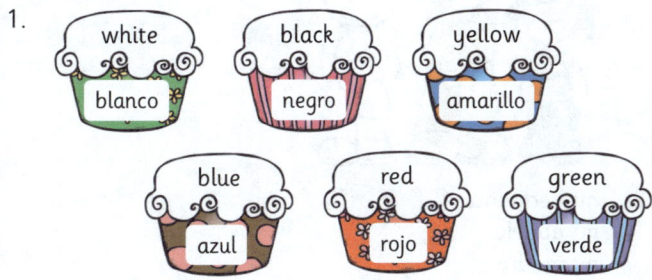

2. verde — green
   negro — black
   blanco — white
   rojo — red
   azul — blue
   amarillo — yellow

3.

Answers

4.
```
q a s e g l g p g f
v r b l a n c o a m
e o n k g d a h z x
r j   n e g r o u g
d o e e o f b o g l h
e   e g j v p f j g r
g m a m a r i l l o
```

An Extra Challenge
balloons: verde
party hats: amarillo
cake icing: blanco

Pages 12-13 — My family

1. You should have coloured:

2. mi hermana
   mi abuela
   mi madre
   mi padre

An Extra Challenge
Mo's <u>mother</u> is called Yasmeen.
Aurelia's <u>grandfather</u> is called Terrence.

Pages 14-15 — Animals

1. fish tank — el pez
   kennel — el perro
   nest — el pájaro

2. Any suitable drawing of a horse, a dog and a rabbit.

3. el pájaro
   el gato
   el conejo
   el pez

An Extra Challenge

2. el gato
3. el pez
4. el pájaro
5. el hámster
6. el perro
7. el caballo

Pages 16-17 — Clothes

1. skirt
   shoes
   dress
   trousers

2. You should have coloured the skirt in red, the trousers in green and the T-shirt in blue.

Answers

3.

4. b) el jersey
   c) la camiseta
   d) los zapatos
   e) el vestido
   f) los pantalones

   An Extra Challenge
   Khadija — el vestido, los calcetines, los zapatos.
   Any suitable list of clothes you are wearing, e.g.
   la camiseta, los pantalones, los zapatos.

Pages 18-19 — Snowy shuffle

You should have matched:
Luisa — the red shoes, the pencil, the chocolate.
Manuel — the green apple, the yellow ruler, the blue socks.
Camila — the sandwich, the purple trousers, the rubber.

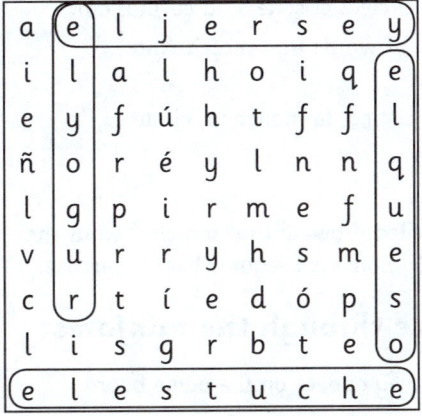

Pages 20-21 — What do you like doing?

1. Me gusta leer —

   Me gusta ver la tele. —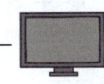

   Me gusta jugar al fútbol. —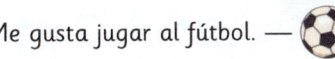

2. Axel likes <u>reading</u>.
   Carys likes <u>swimming</u>.

3. You should have circled:

An Extra Challenge
Sahar — Me gusta escuchar música.
Karine — Me gusta bailar.
Pascal — Me gusta jugar al fútbol.
Any suitable answer, e.g. 'Me gusta nadar y leer.'

Pages 22-23 — Food

1. el queso
   el yogur
   la manzana

2. Any suitable drawings of chips, some chocolate and some spaghetti.

3. el yogur —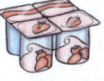

   el queso —

   la manzana —

4. You should have coloured in:

An Extra Challenge
el choco<u>la</u>te
el bocadi<u>ll</u>o
la <u>ma</u>nzana
el qu<u>e</u>so
The ingredient is: lime

Pages 24-25 — In my pencil case

1. You should have coloured in: la goma, el lápiz, la regla.

2. el bolígrafo — pen
   el sacapuntas — pencil sharpener
   la regla — ruler
   el estuche — pencil case
   la goma — rubber

3. a) la regla
   b) la goma
   c) el bolígrafo

Answers

An Extra Challenge

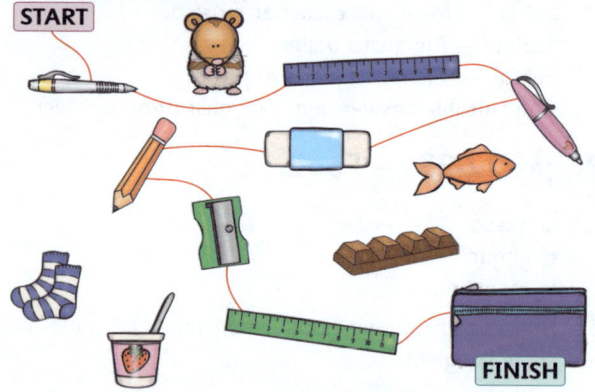

Any sensible list, e.g. el lápiz, la regla, la goma.

Pages 26-27 — Where do you live?

1. Vivo en una casa.

    Vivo cerca del mar.

    Vivo en el campo.

    Vivo en un castillo.

    Vivo en la ciudad.

2. You should have coloured:

    Vivo en la ciudad.

    Vivo en el campo.

    Vivo cerca del mar.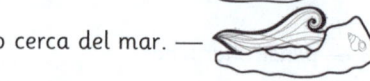

An Extra Challenge
Any sensible drawing of a house in the countryside.
Any sensible sentence about where you live, e.g. Vivo en un piso en la ciudad.

Pages 28-29 — My house

1. el cuarto de baño — the bathroom
   la cocina — the kitchen
   el dormitorio — the bedroom
   el comedor — the dining room

2. el salón
   el comedor
   la cocina

3. el dormitorio
   la cocina
   el salón

4. You should have coloured these words in red:
   el, cuarto, de, baño
   You should have coloured these words in blue:
   el, comedor

5. b) el dormitorio
   c) la cocina

An Extra Challenge
el salón
el dormitorio
la cocina

Pages 30-31 — Do you remember?

1. Me llamo [your name].

2.

   From top to bottom: blue, white, red, yellow, green, black.

3. You should have circled: el conejo, la cocina, adiós.

4. Any combination of words that match what you're wearing.

5. You should have circled: la manzana, el queso, las patatas fritas.

Extra Challenge
Any sensible labelled drawing that matches what the crab is saying: My name is Diego. I live in a house.

Page 32 — Race through the rainforest

Answers in the order they appear on the game board:

1. blue
2. Any 3 of the following: la falda, los pantalones, el jersey, el vestido, la camiseta, los zapatos, los calcetines.
3. ¿Qué tal?
4. Any sensible answer, e.g.
   Me gusta jugar al fútbol.
   Me gusta escuchar música.
5. el pájaro
6. Vivo en un castillo.
7. mi hermana
8. rubber
9. uno, dos, tres, cuatro, cinco
10. in the countryside